Indian Girls

Hot Sexy Indian Lingerie Girls Models Pictures

By **PHOTO ART LOVER**

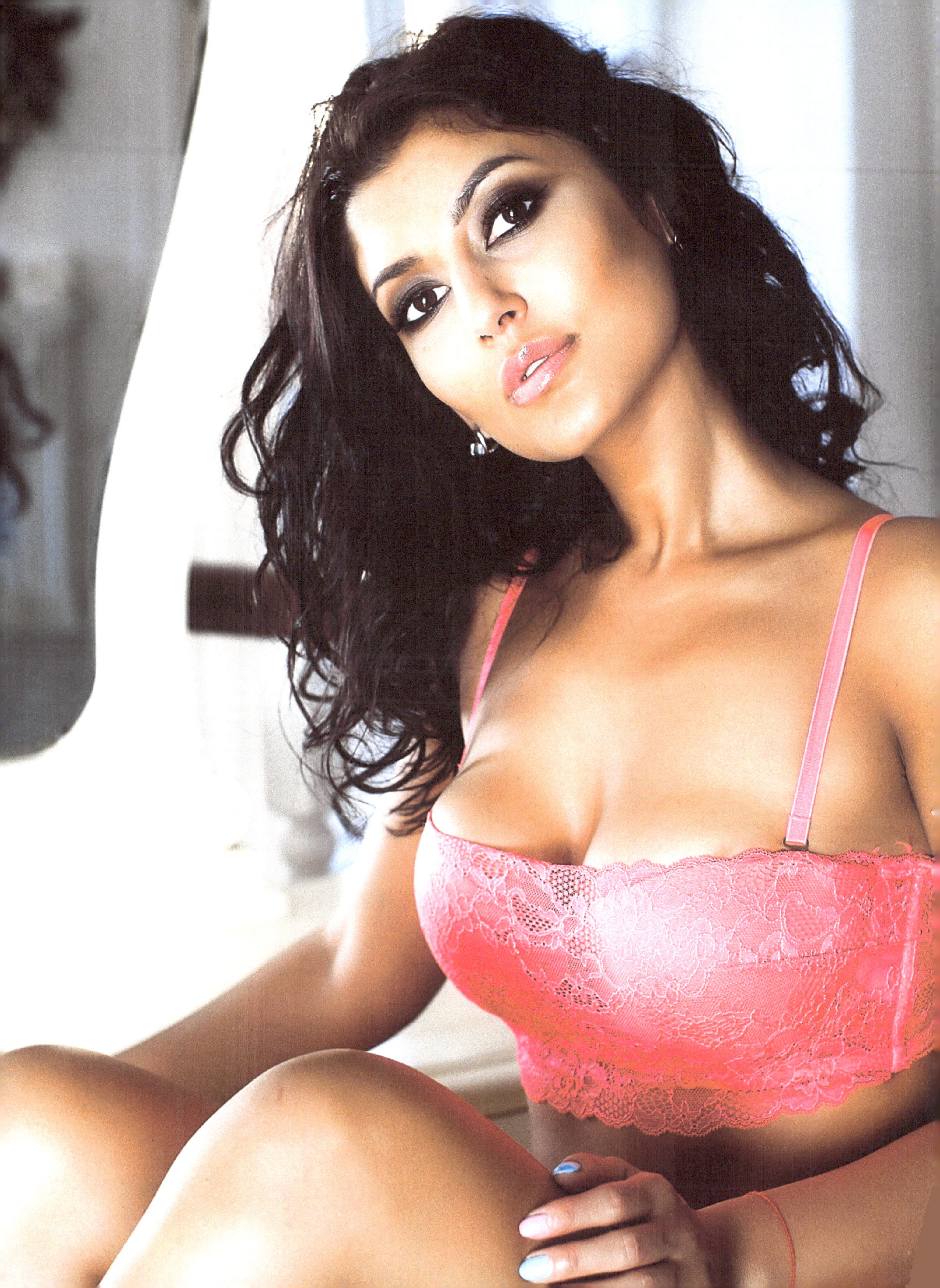

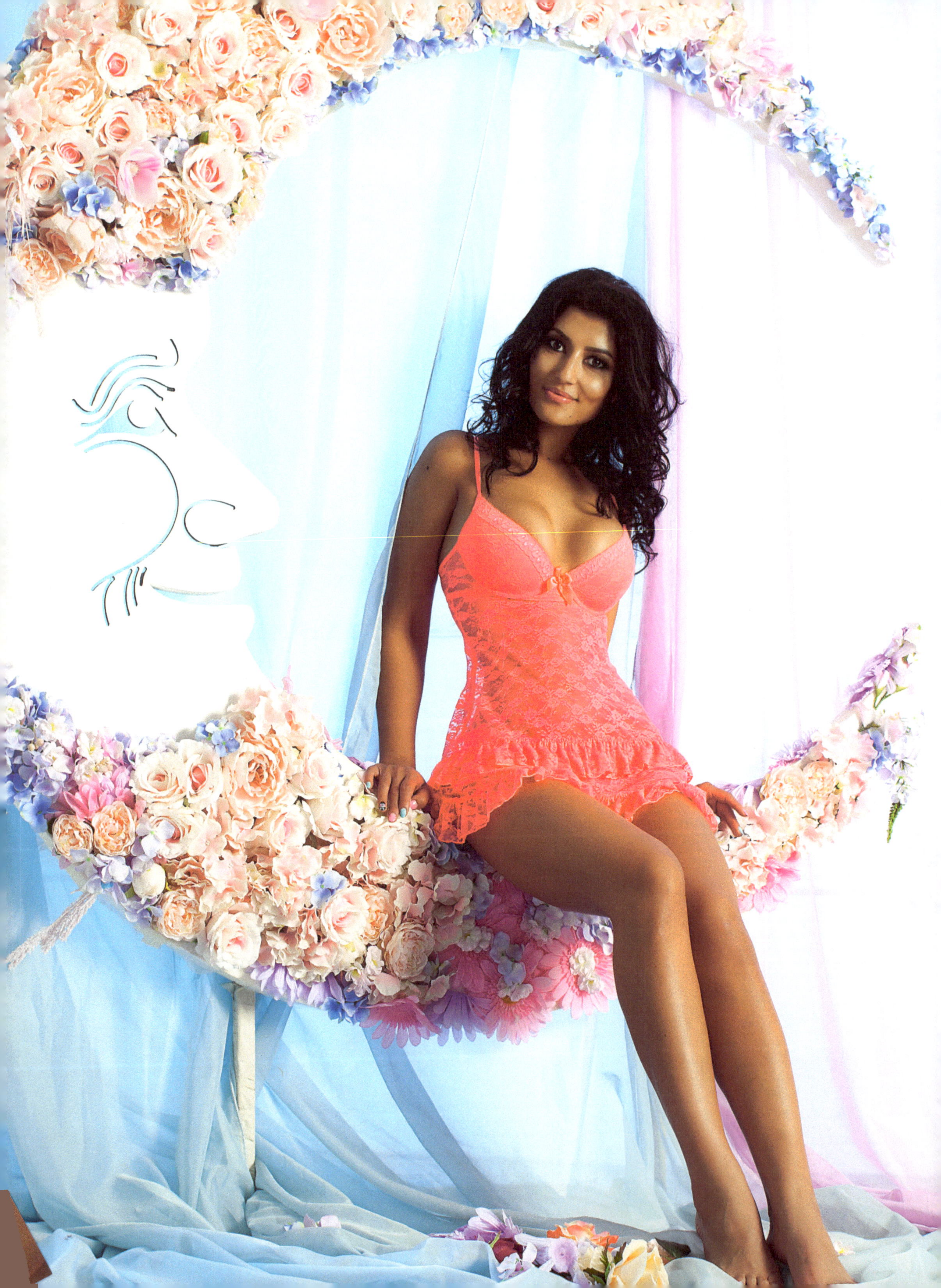

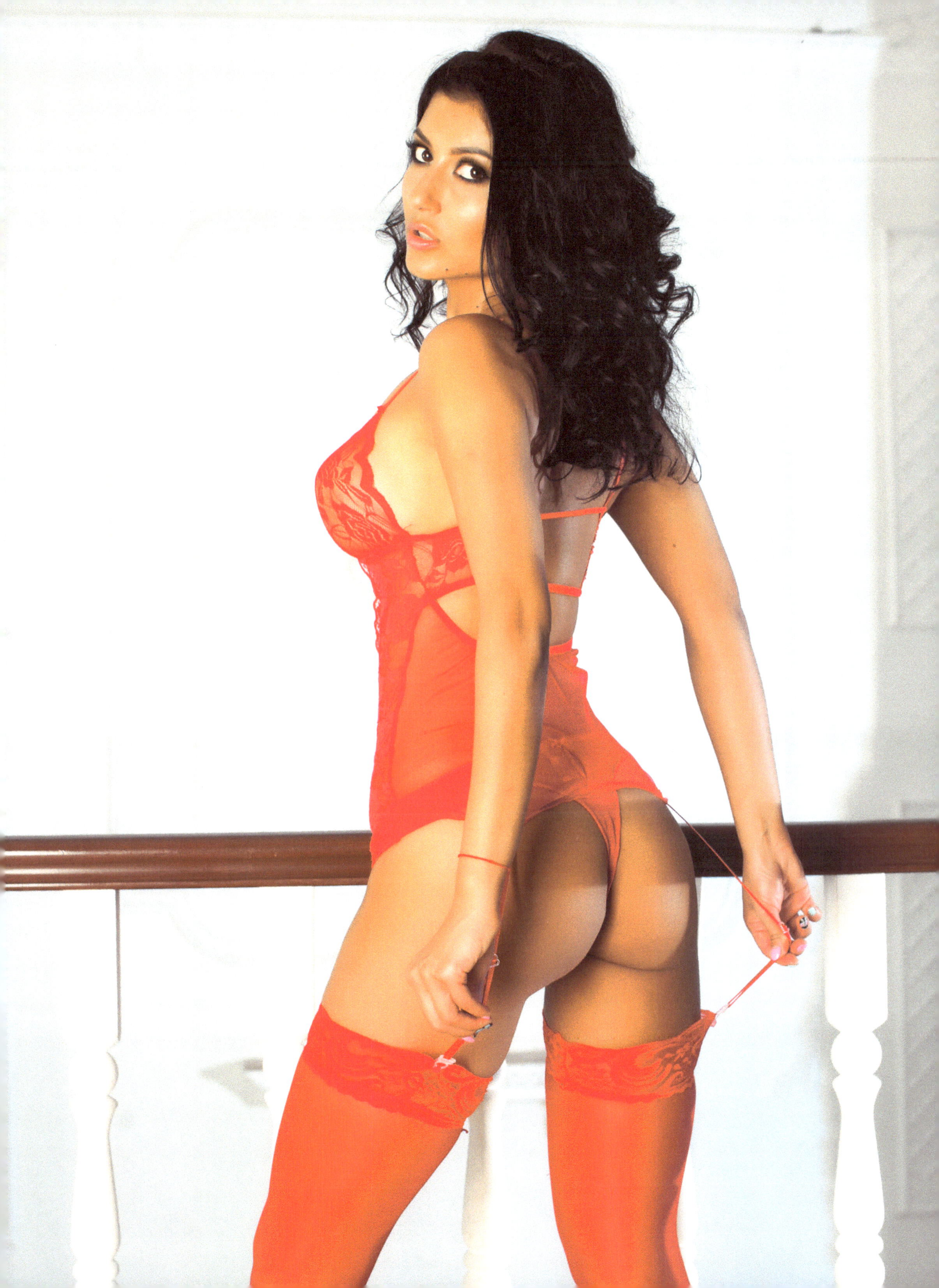

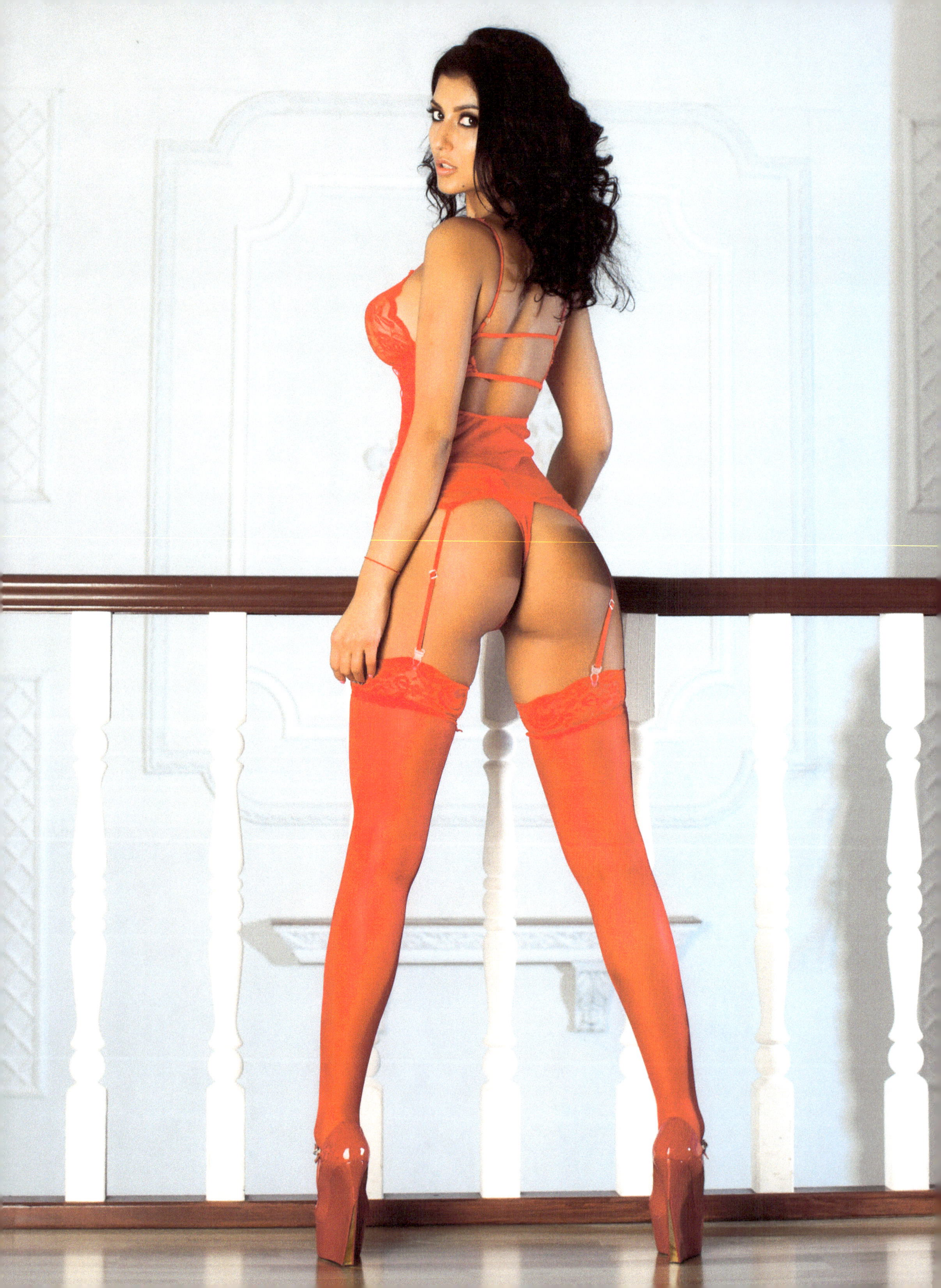

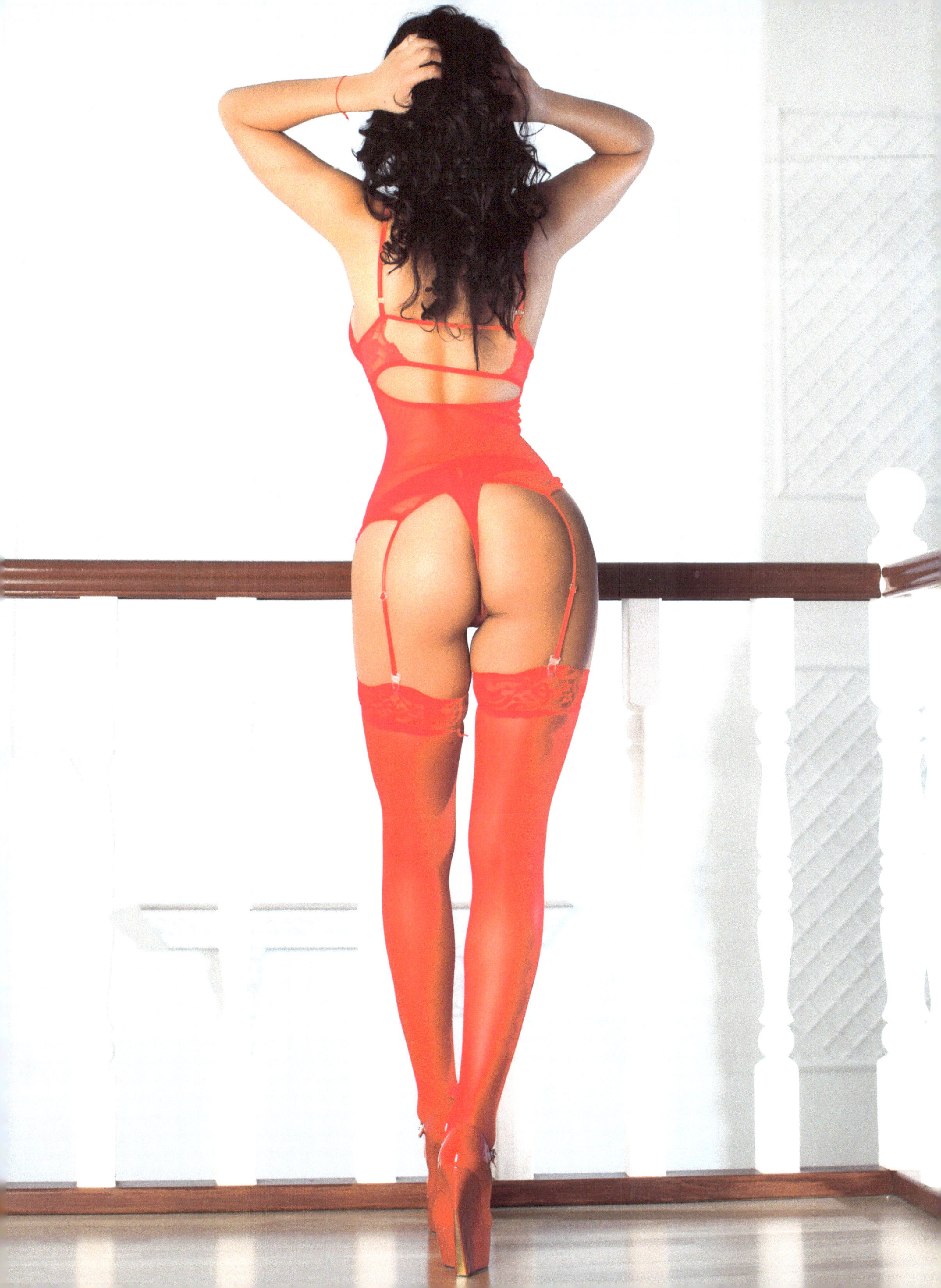

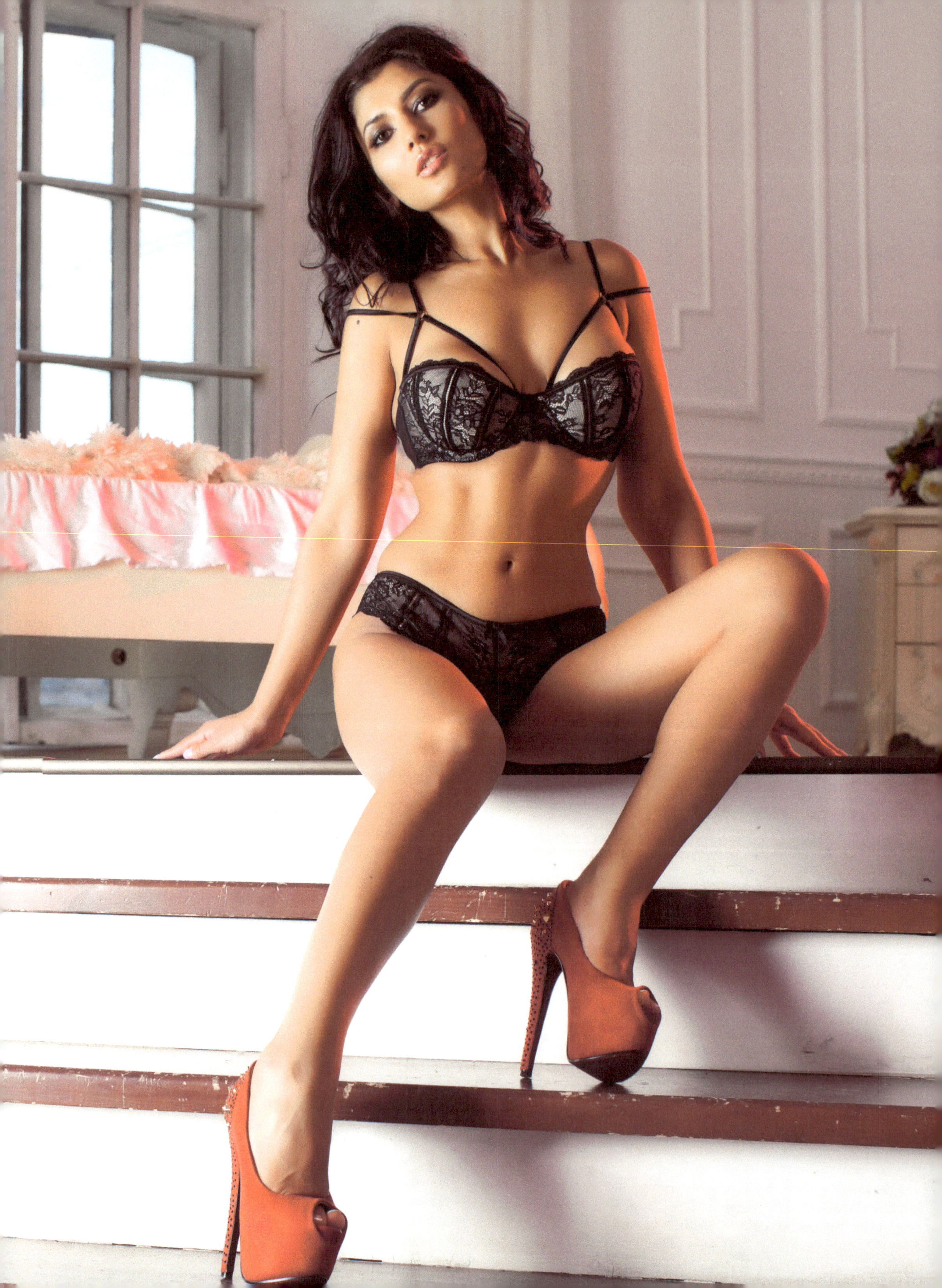

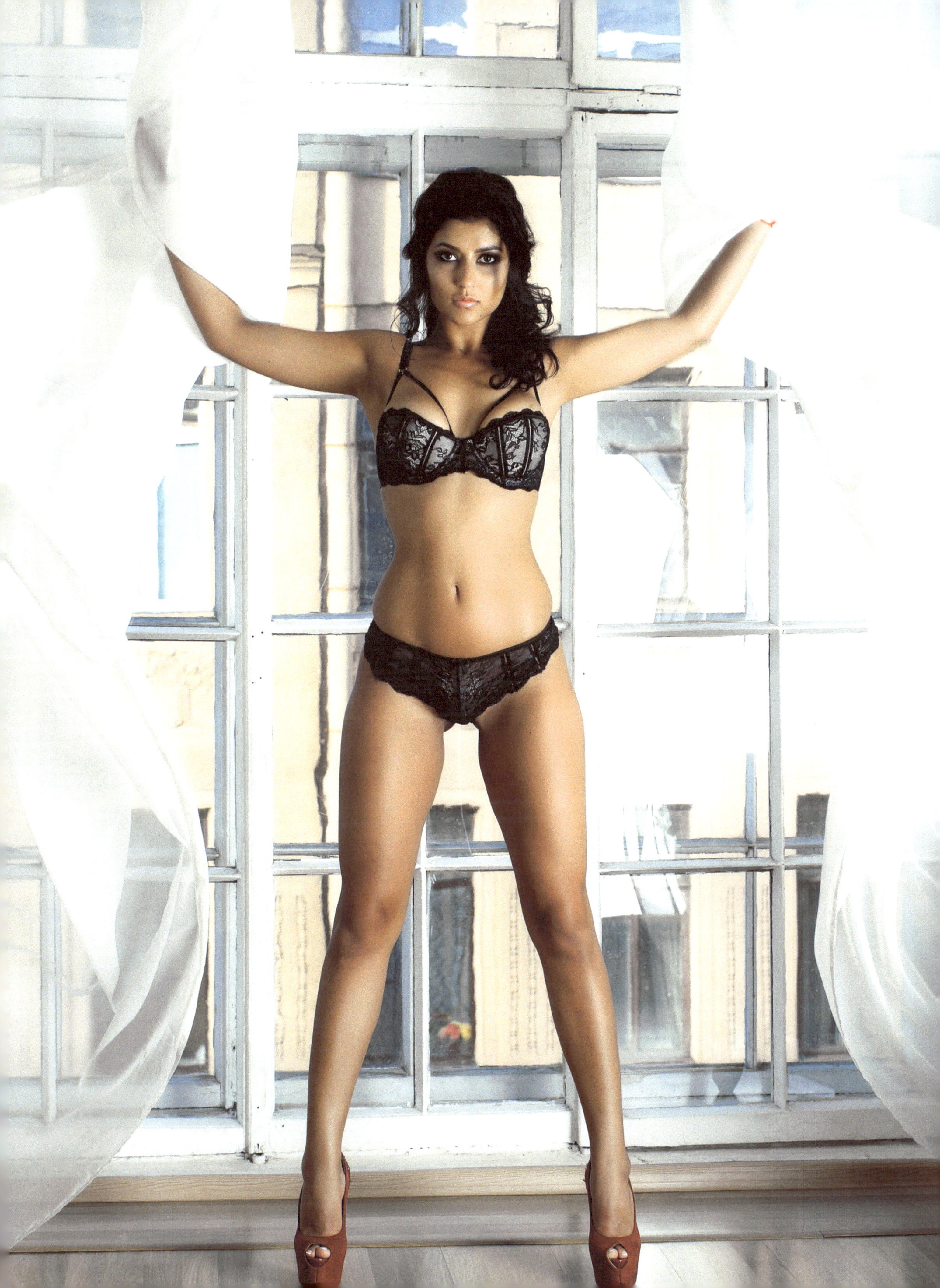

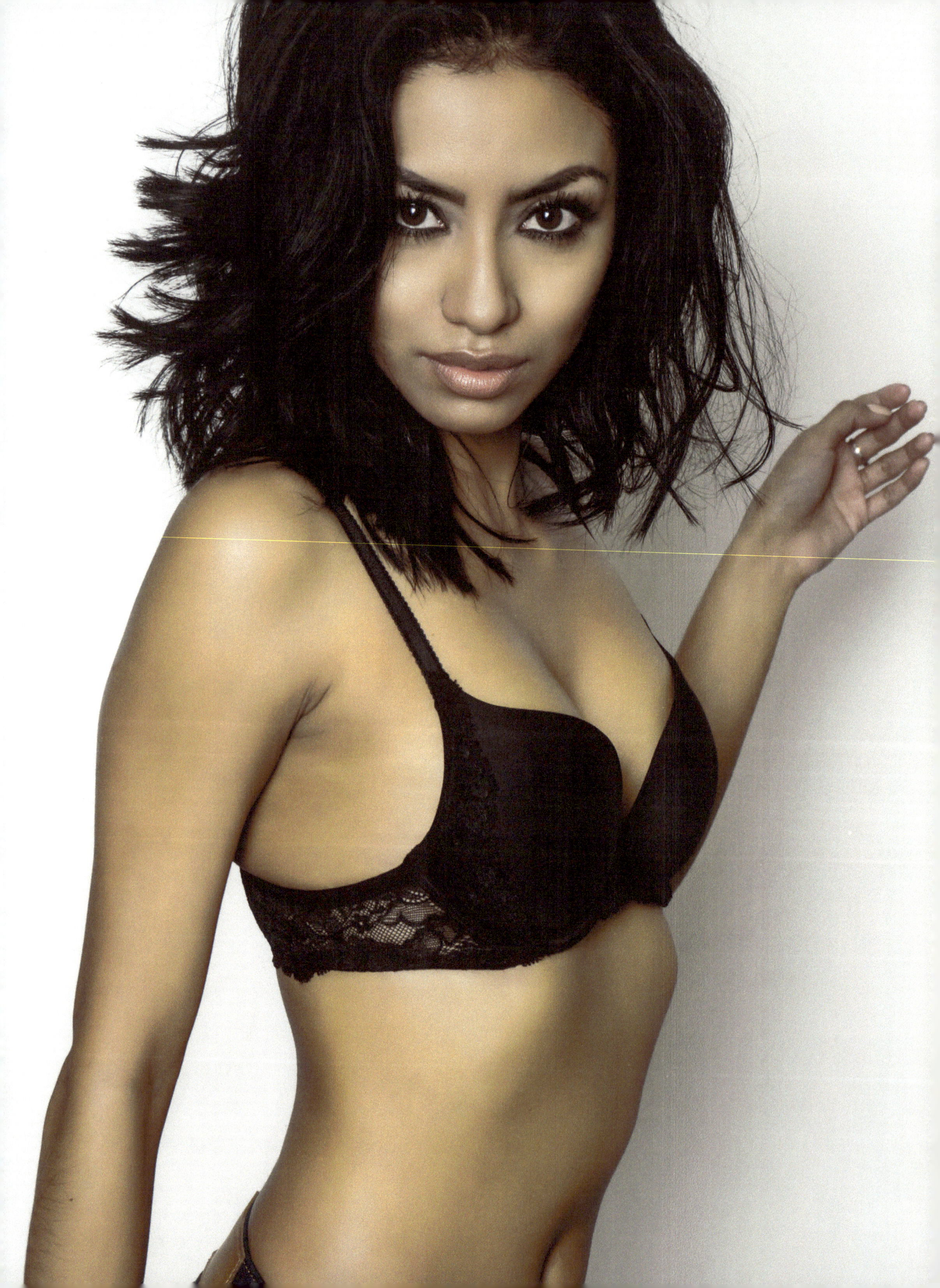

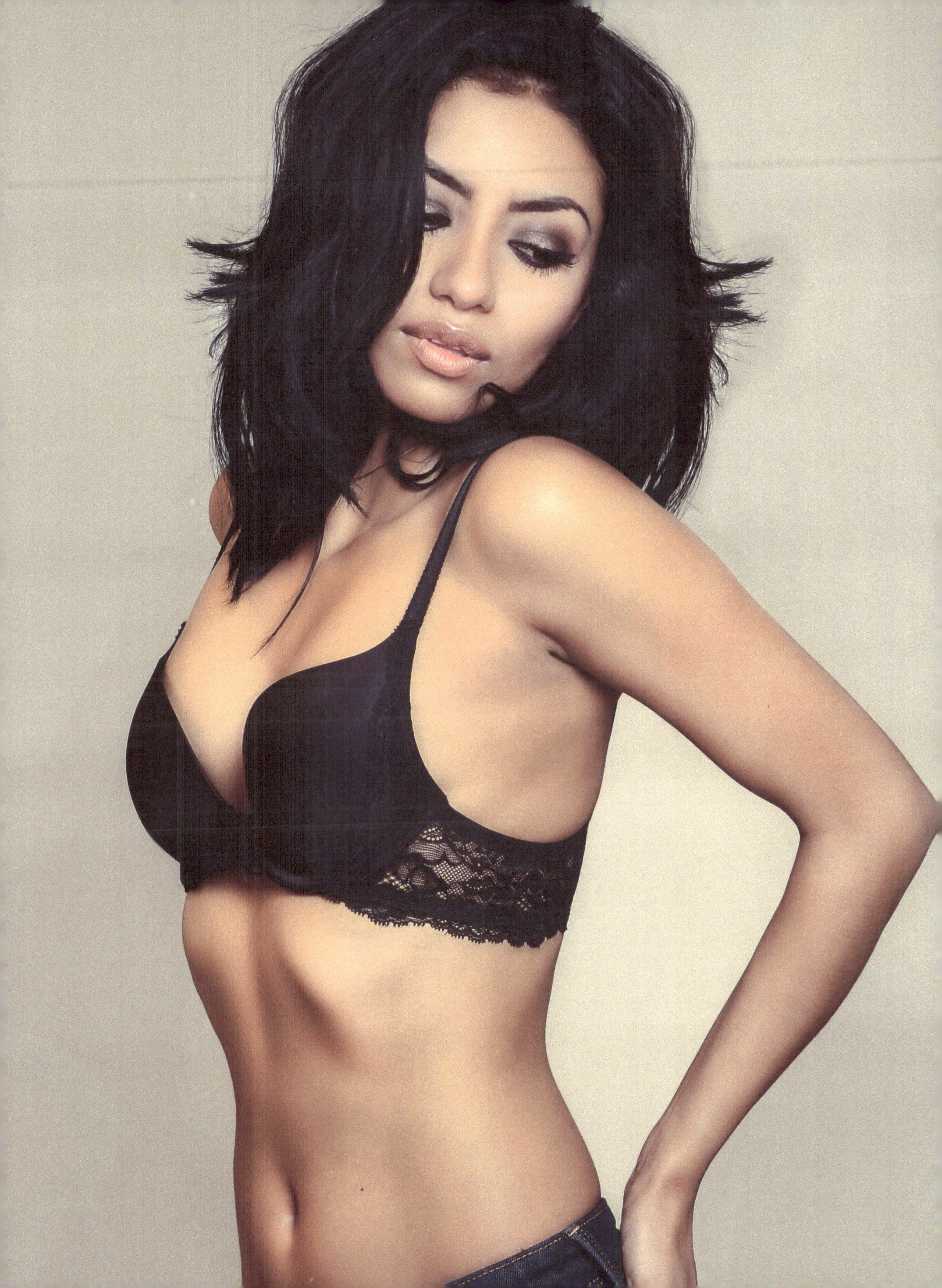

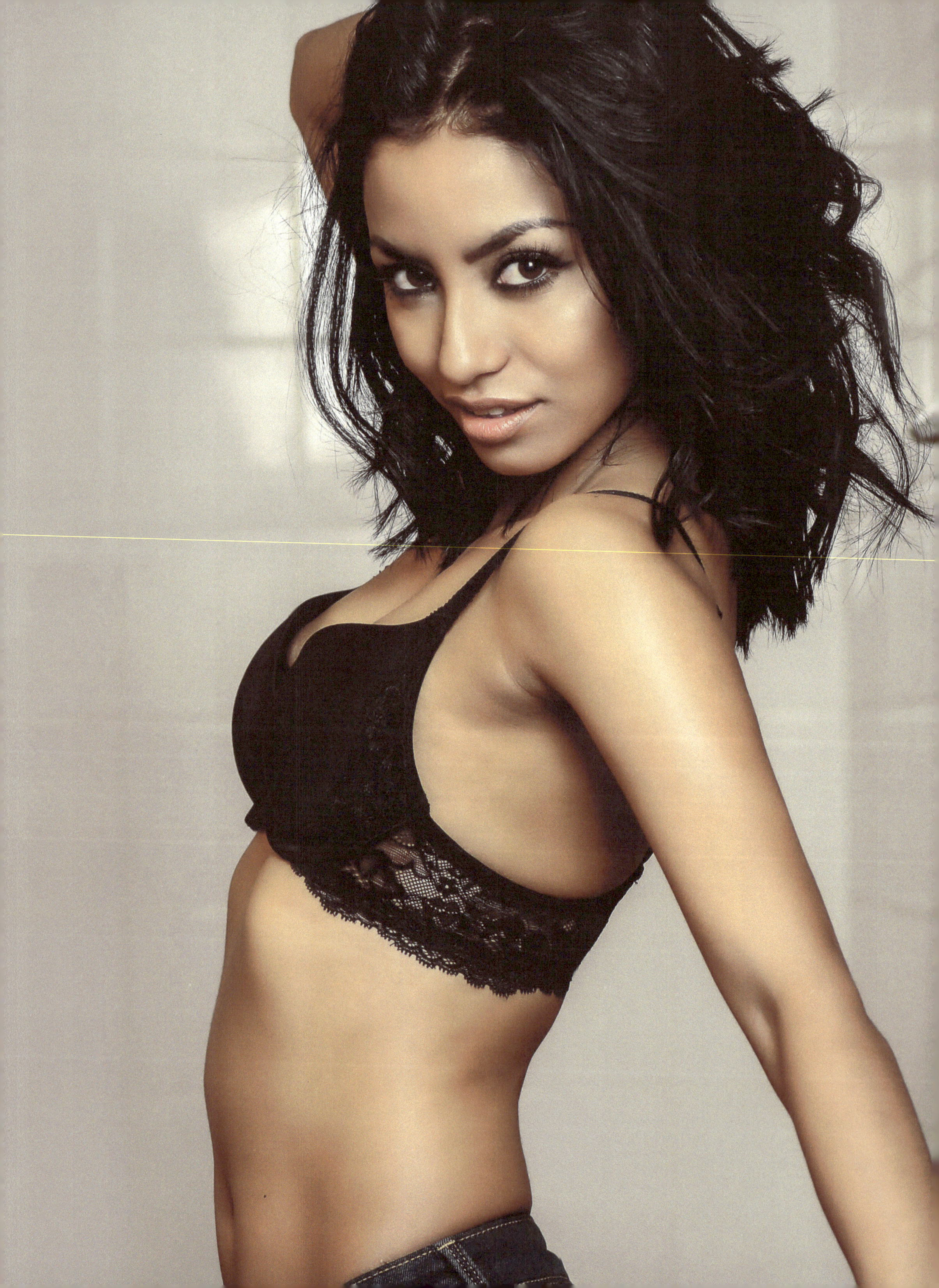

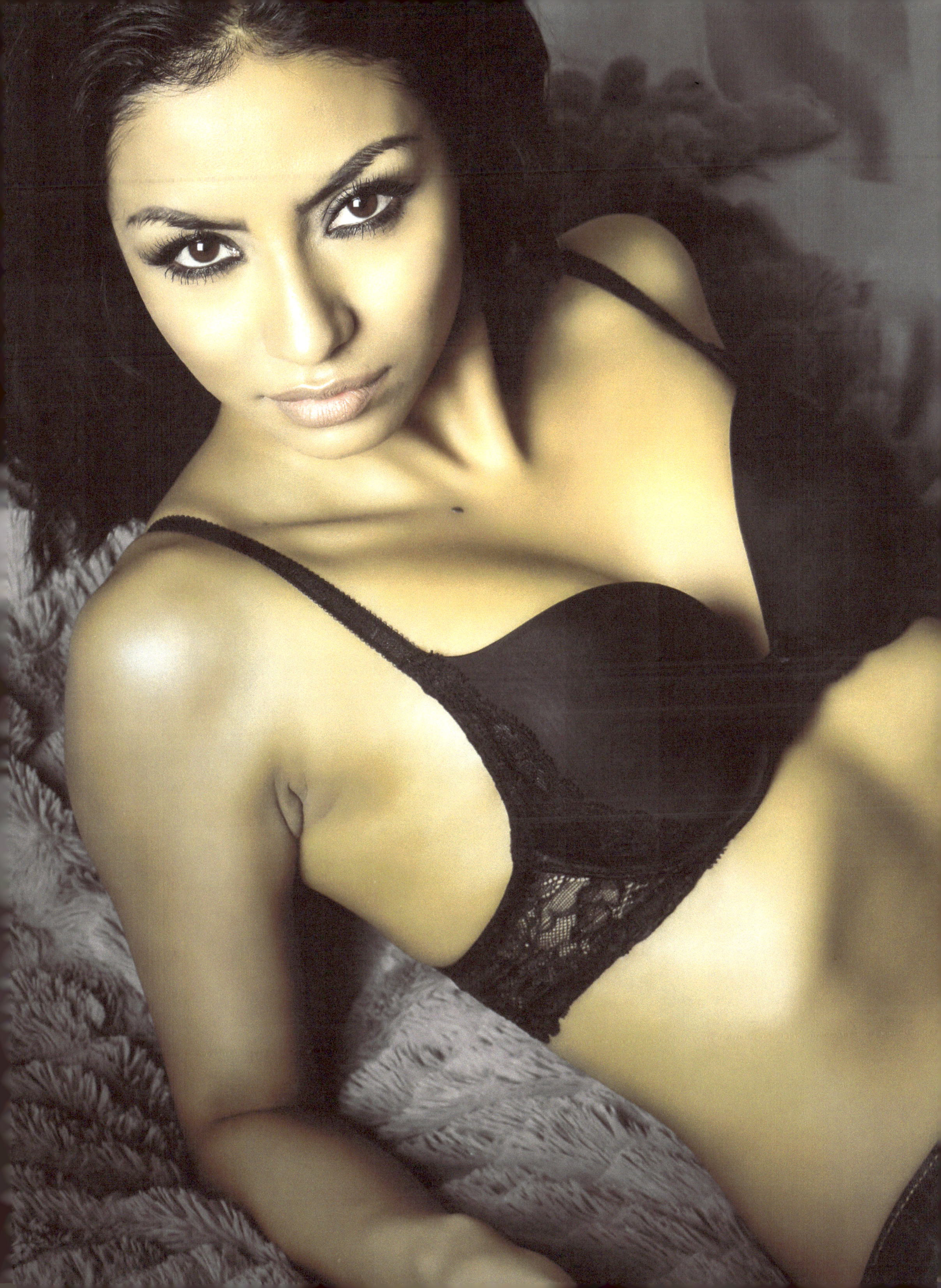

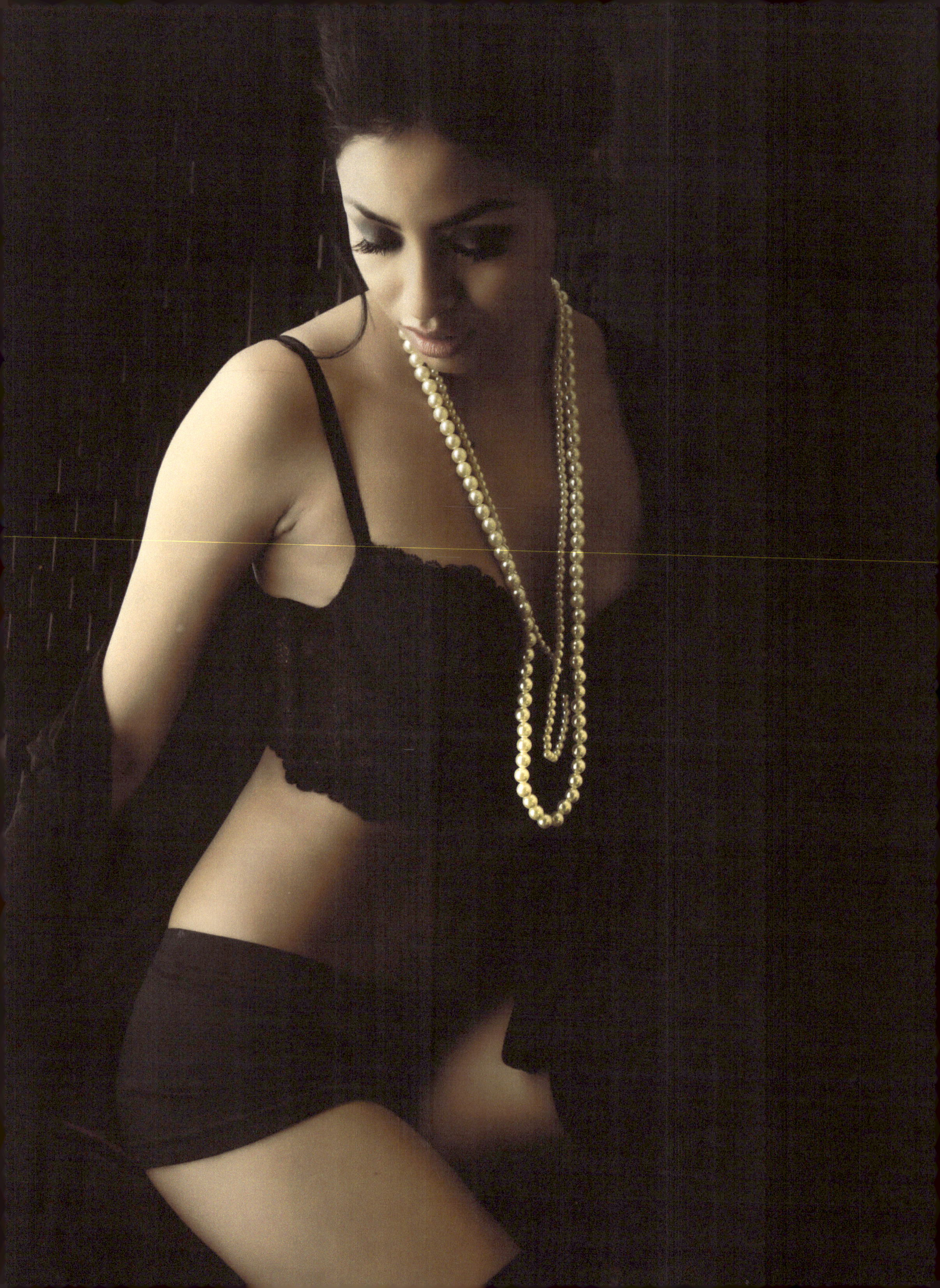

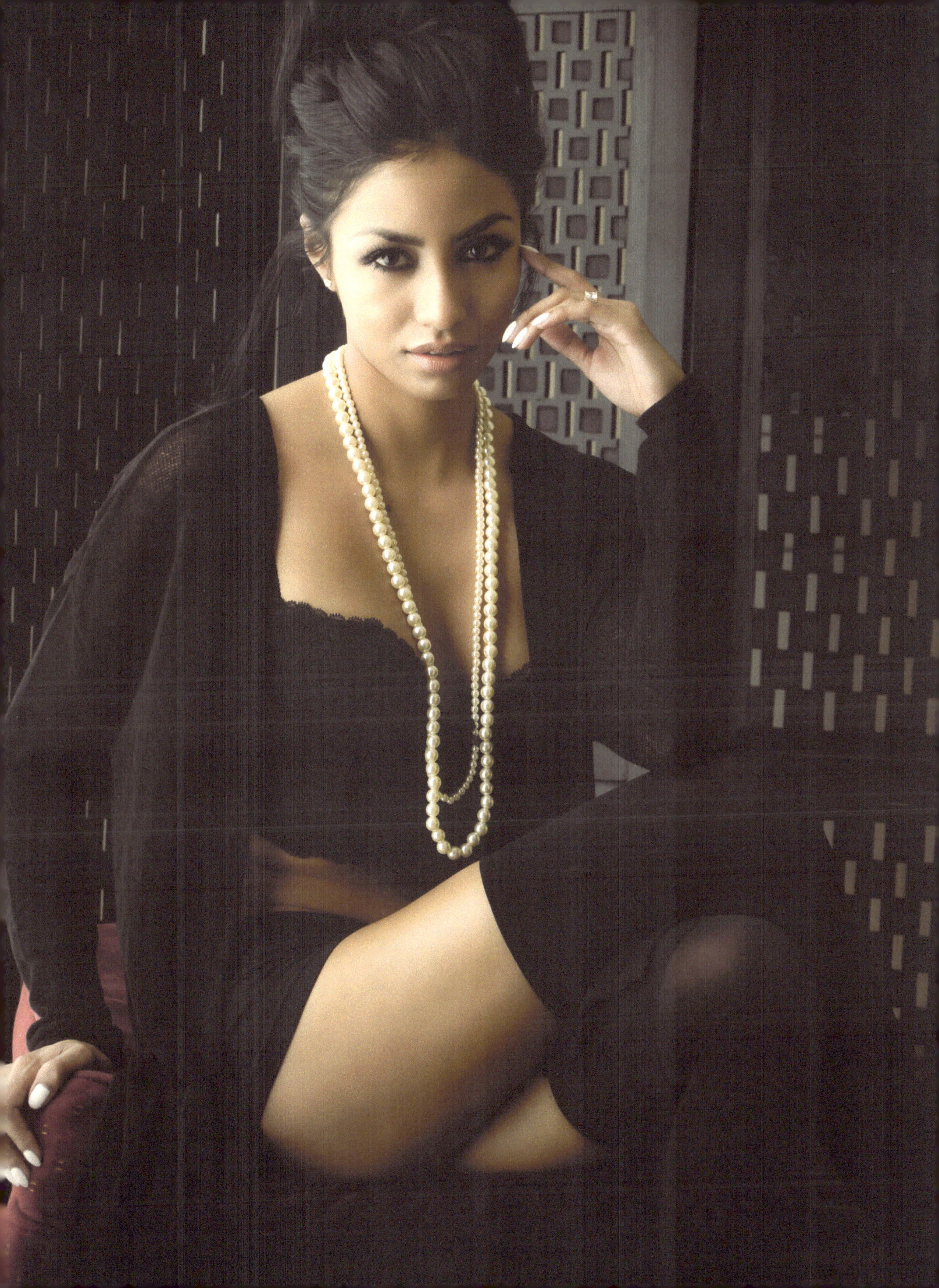

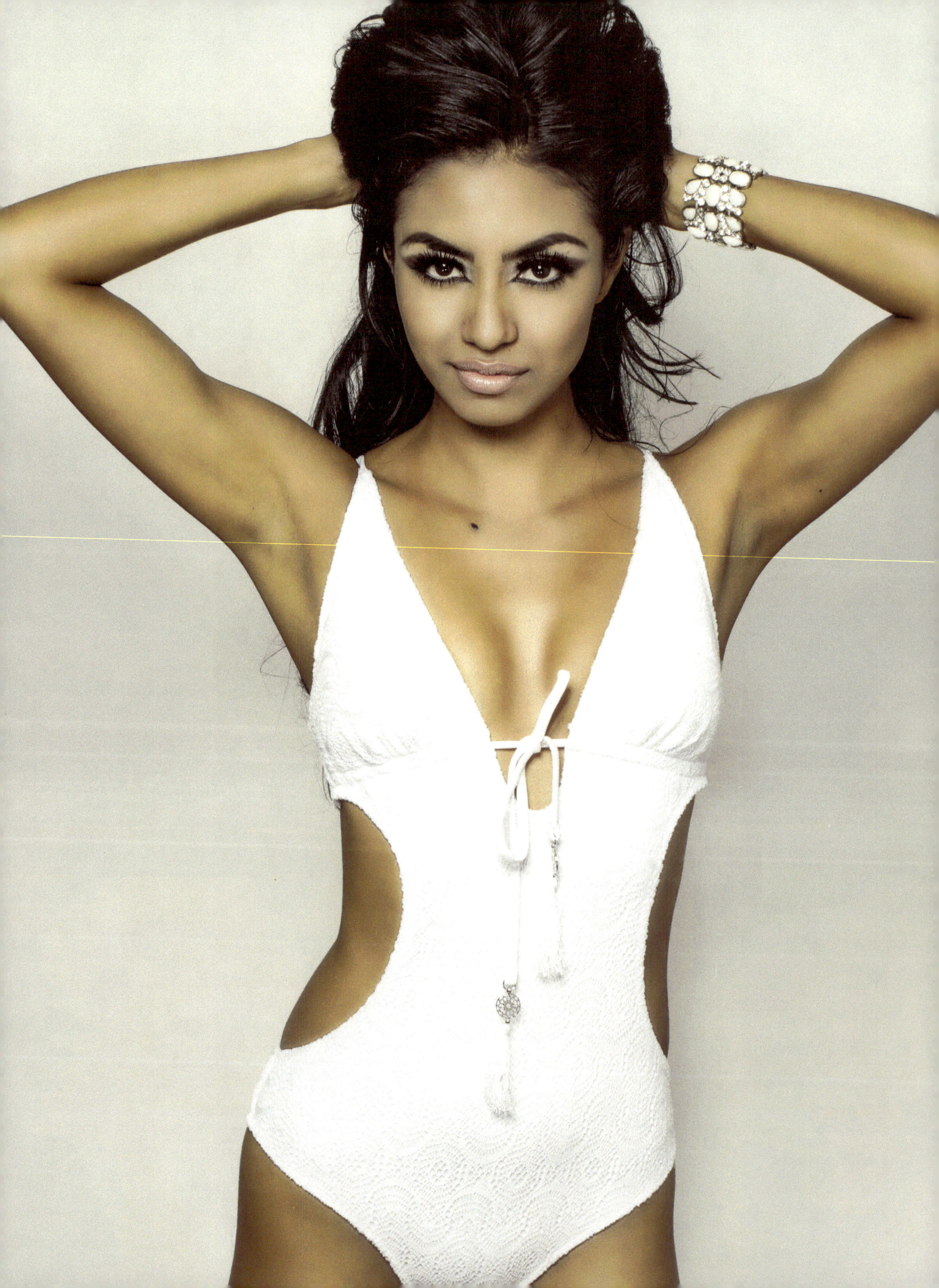

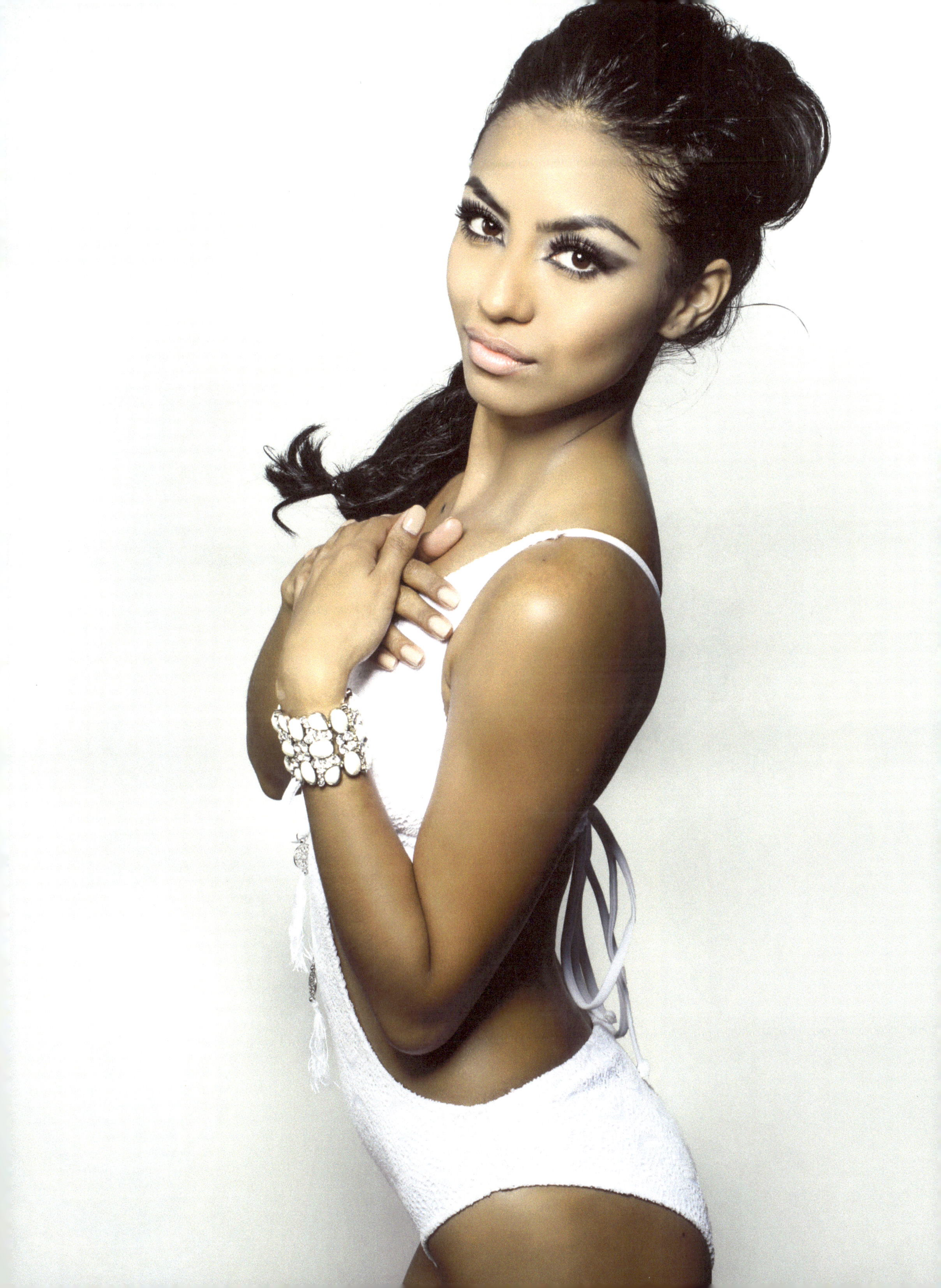

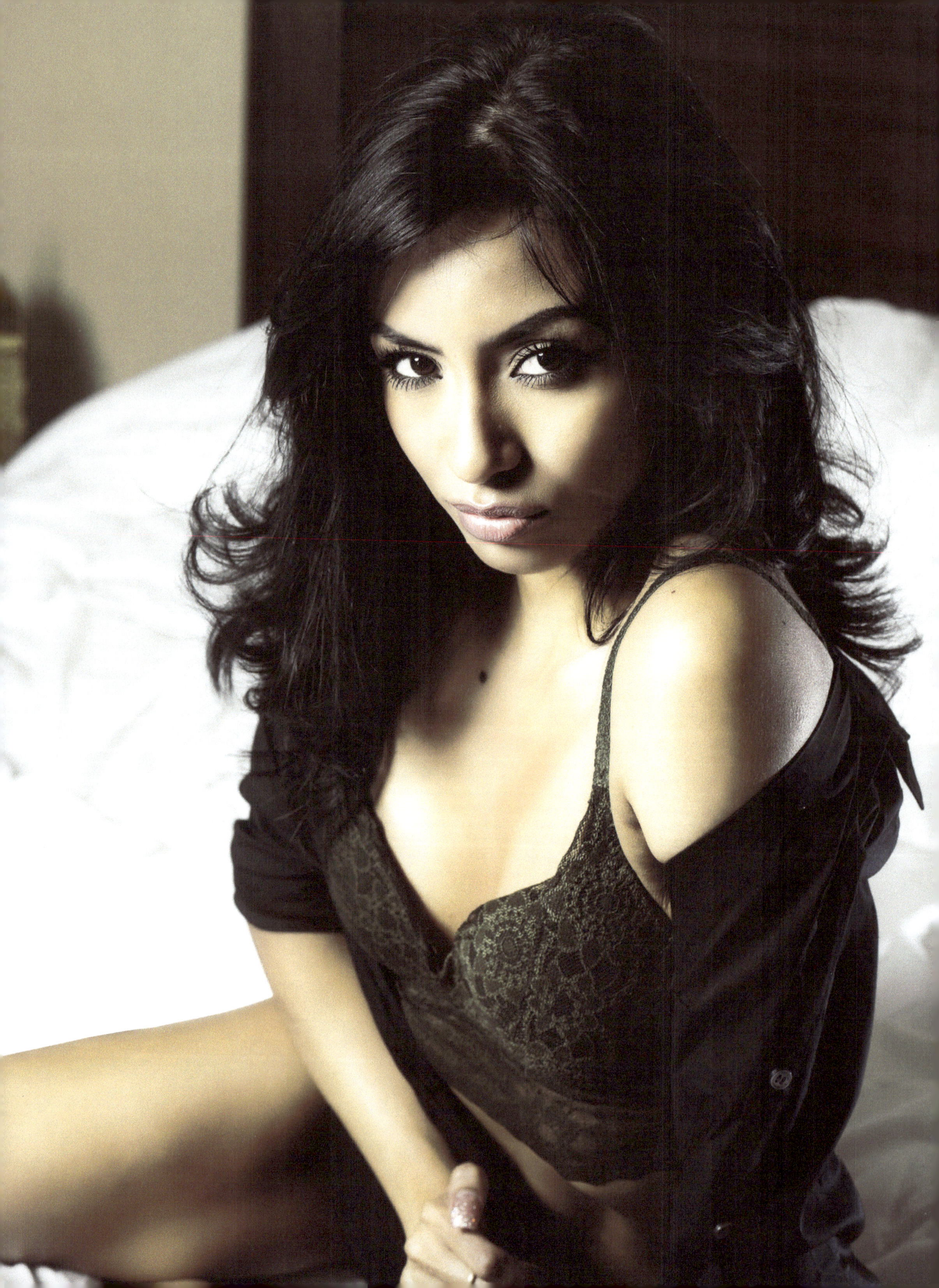

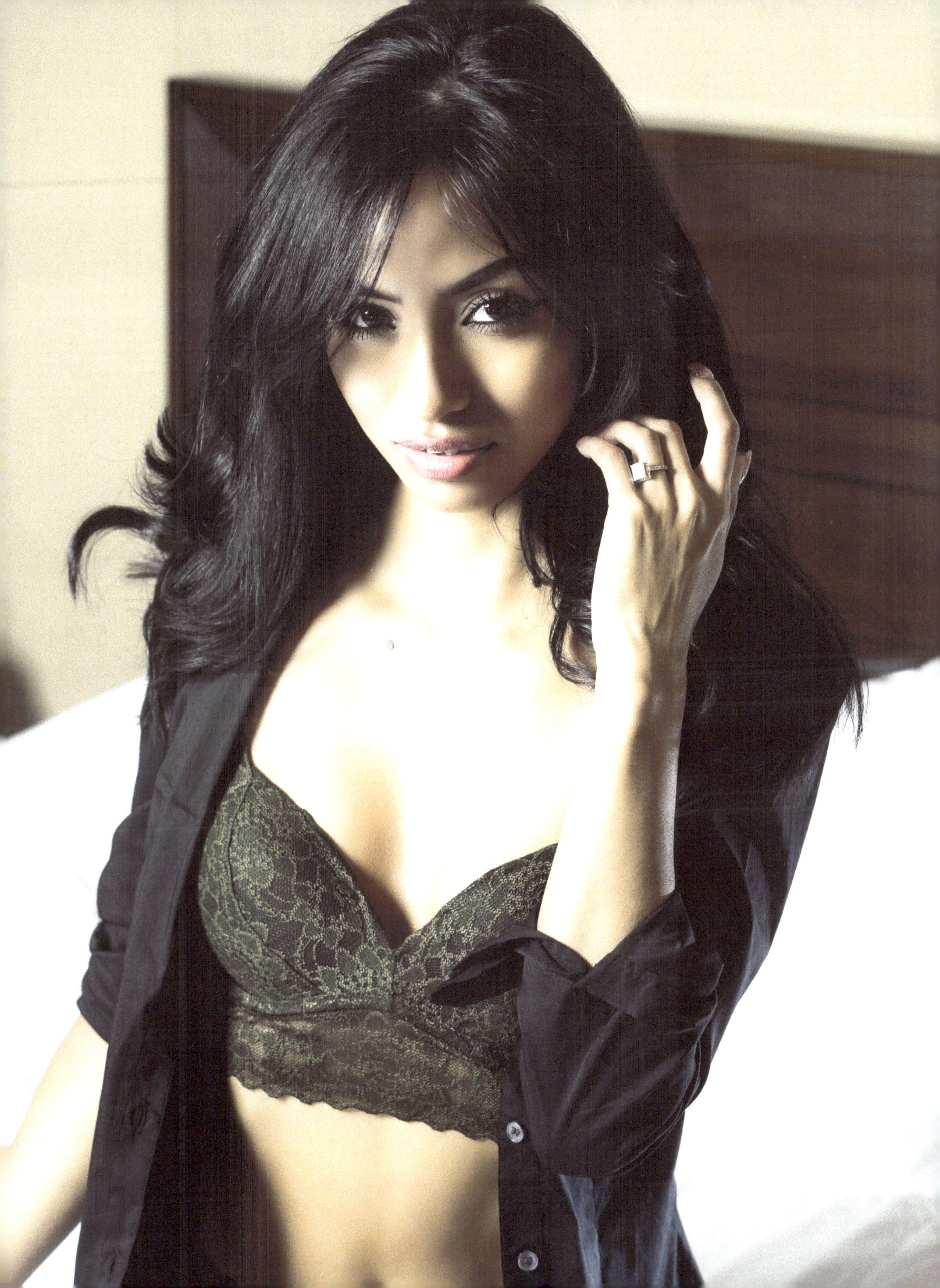

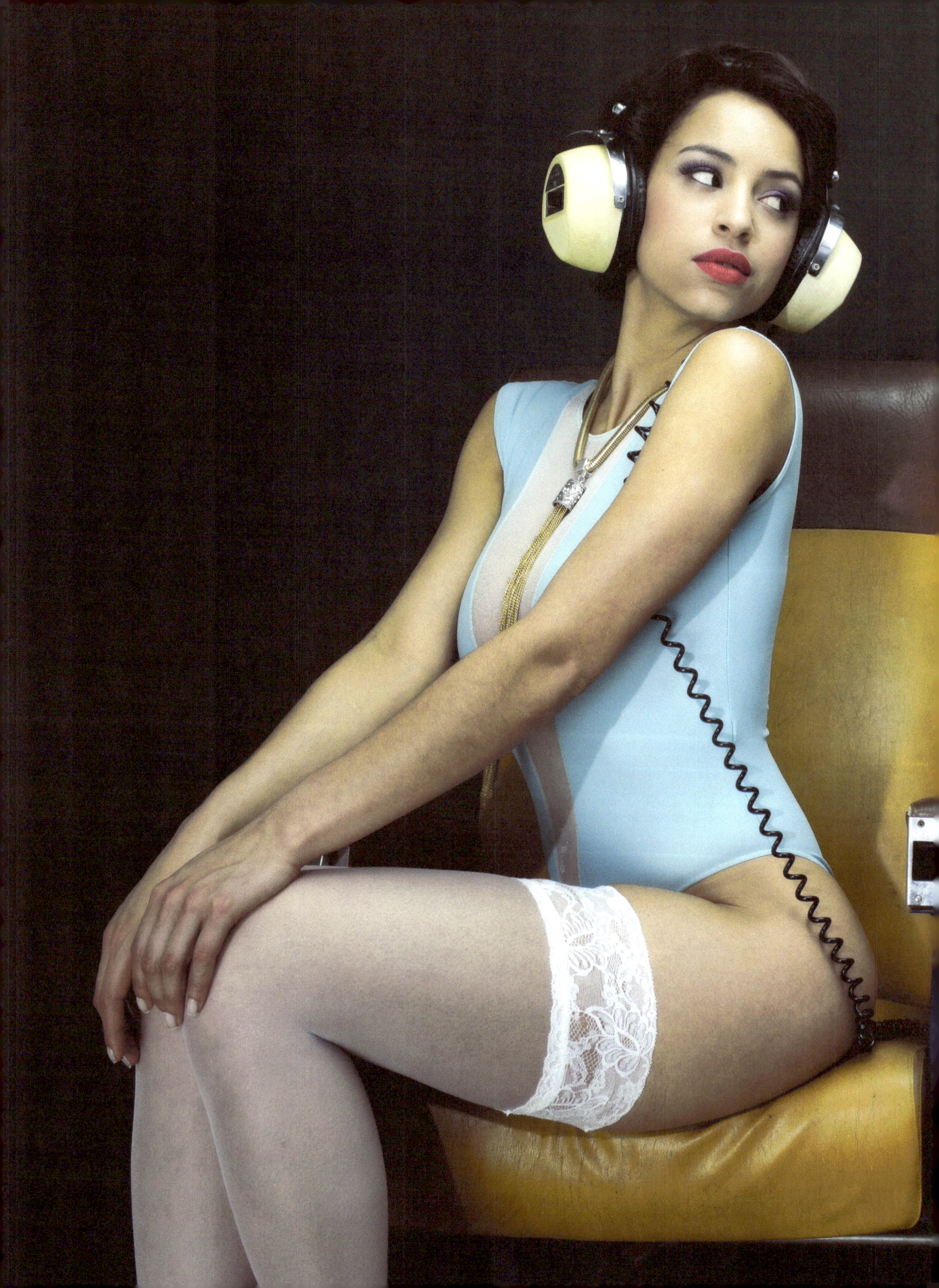

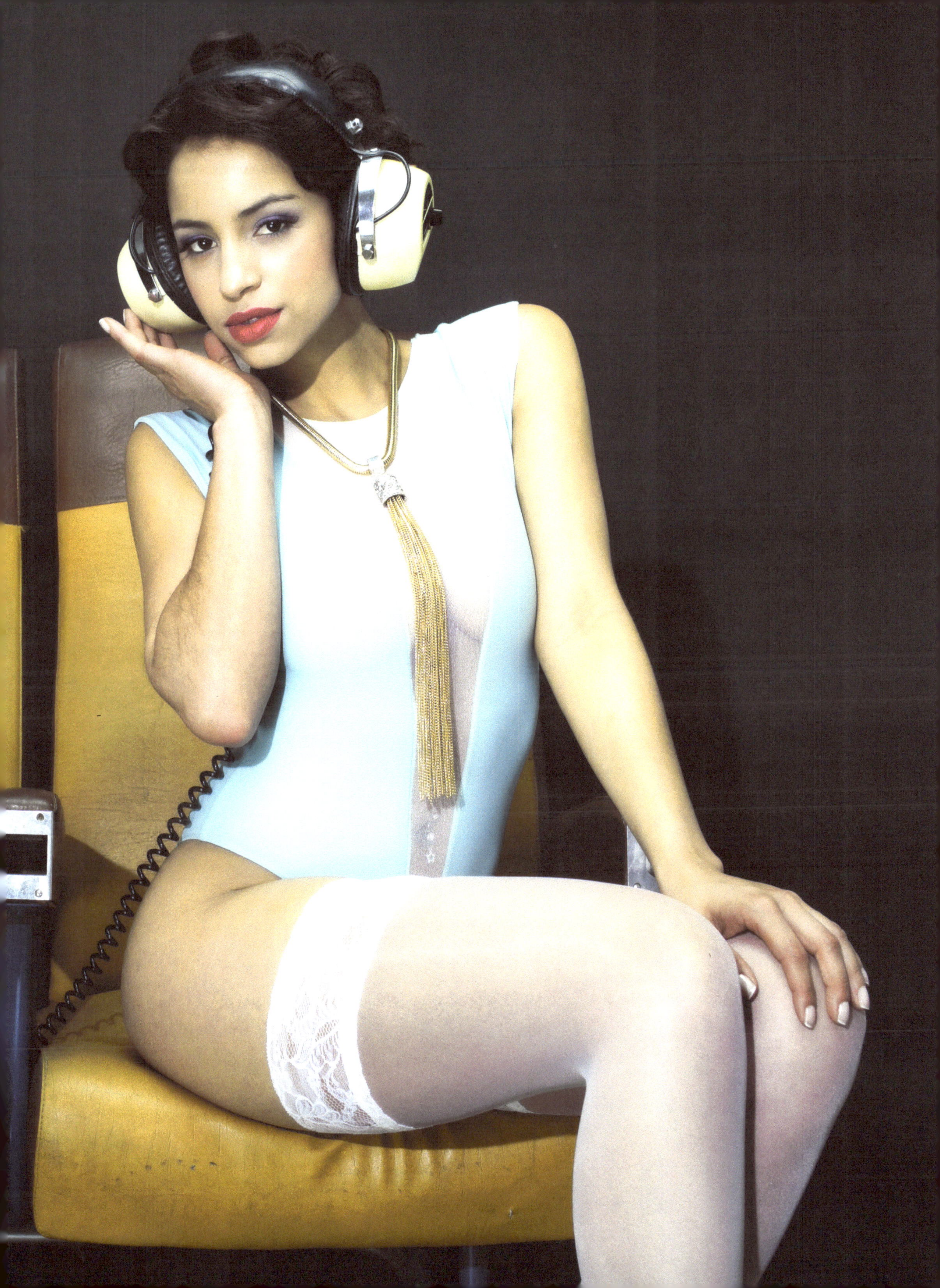

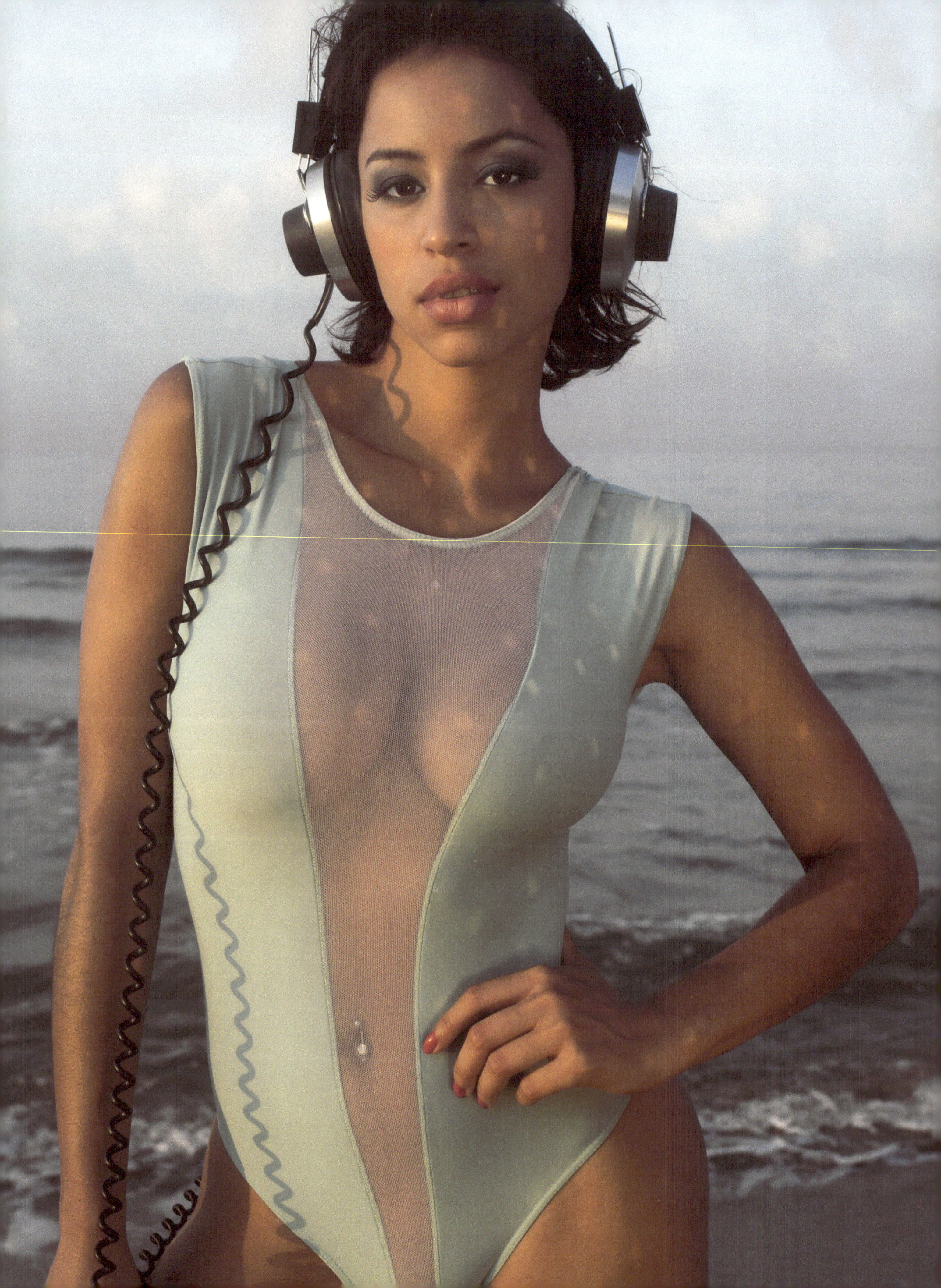

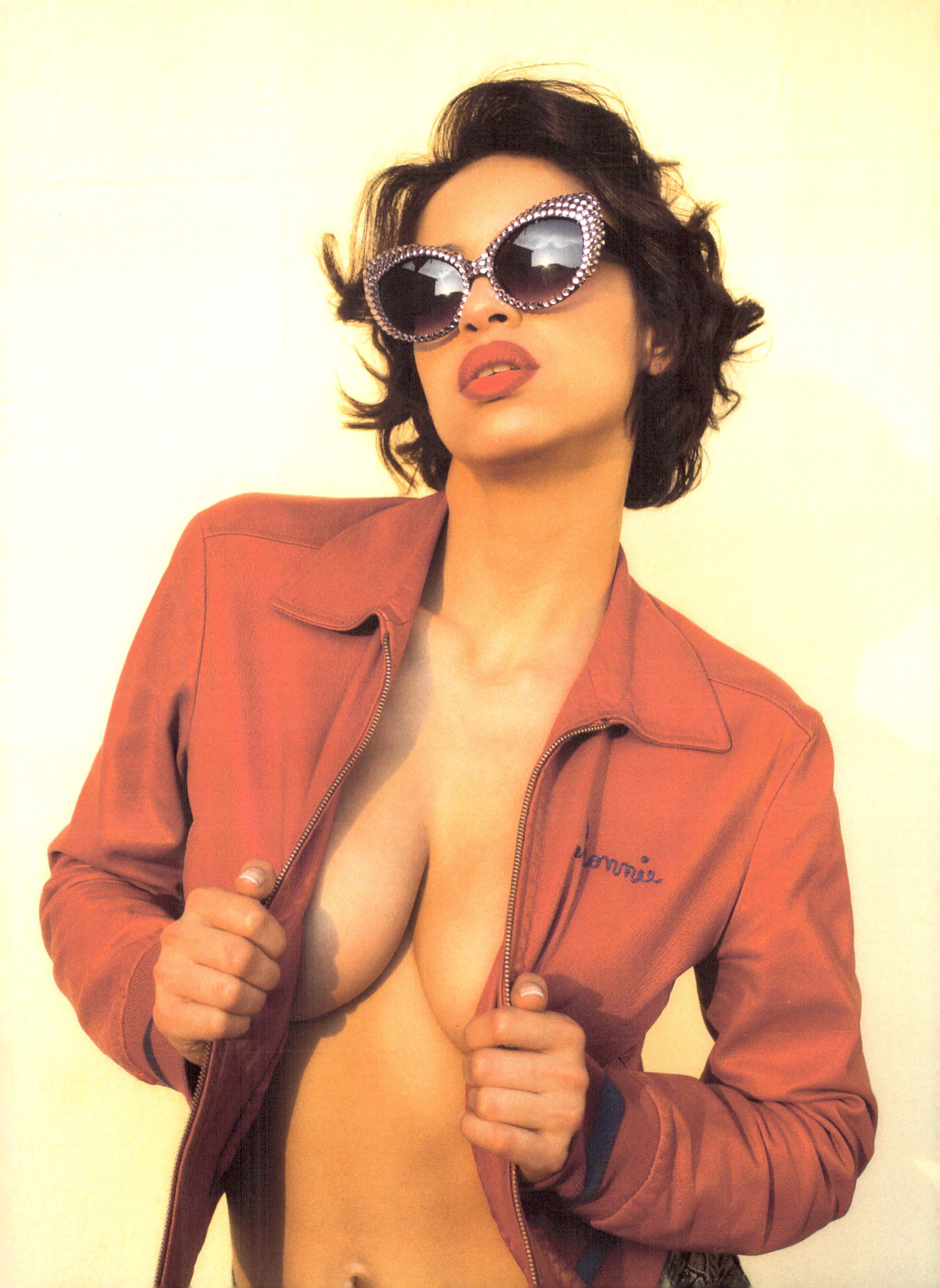

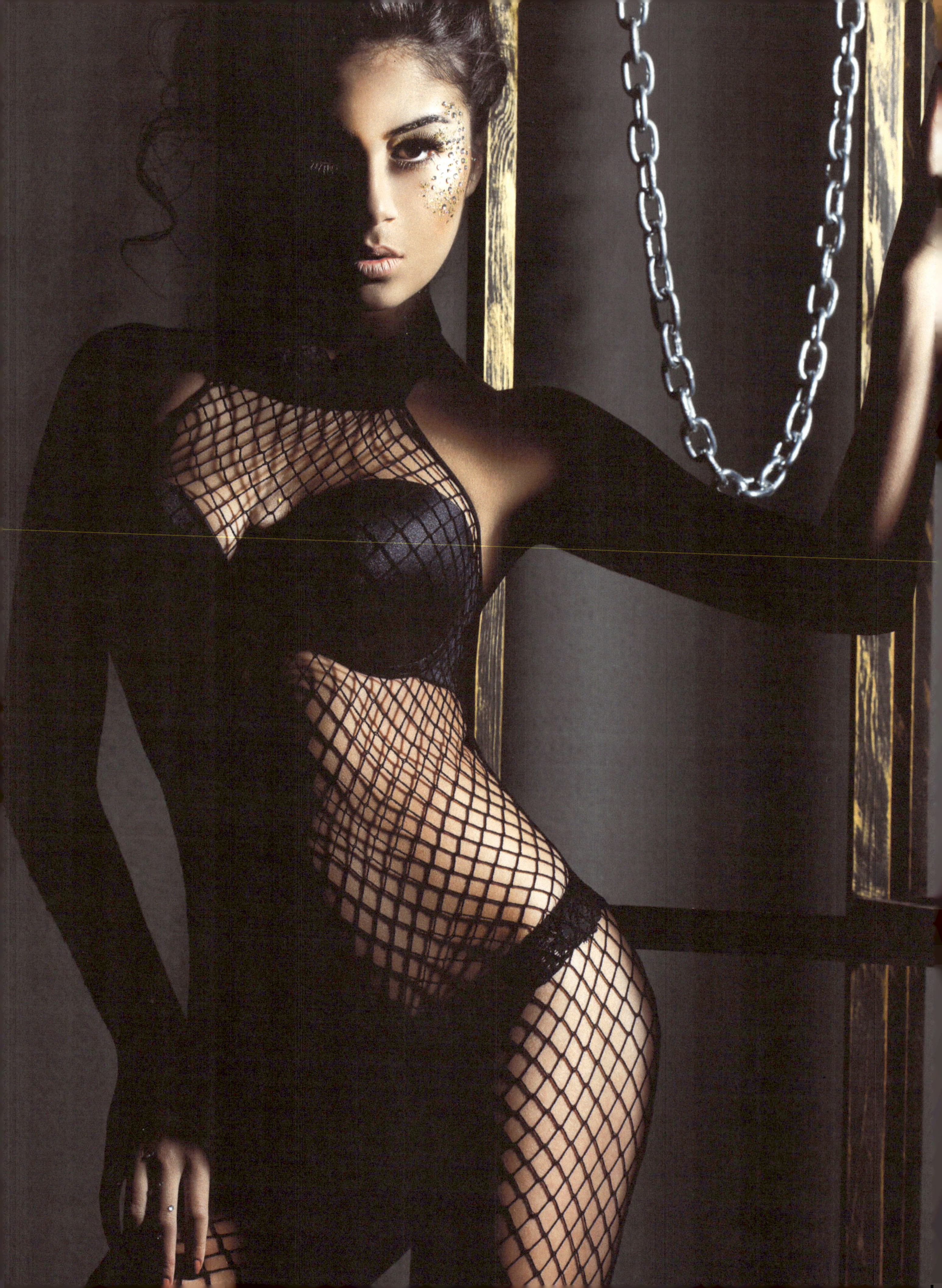

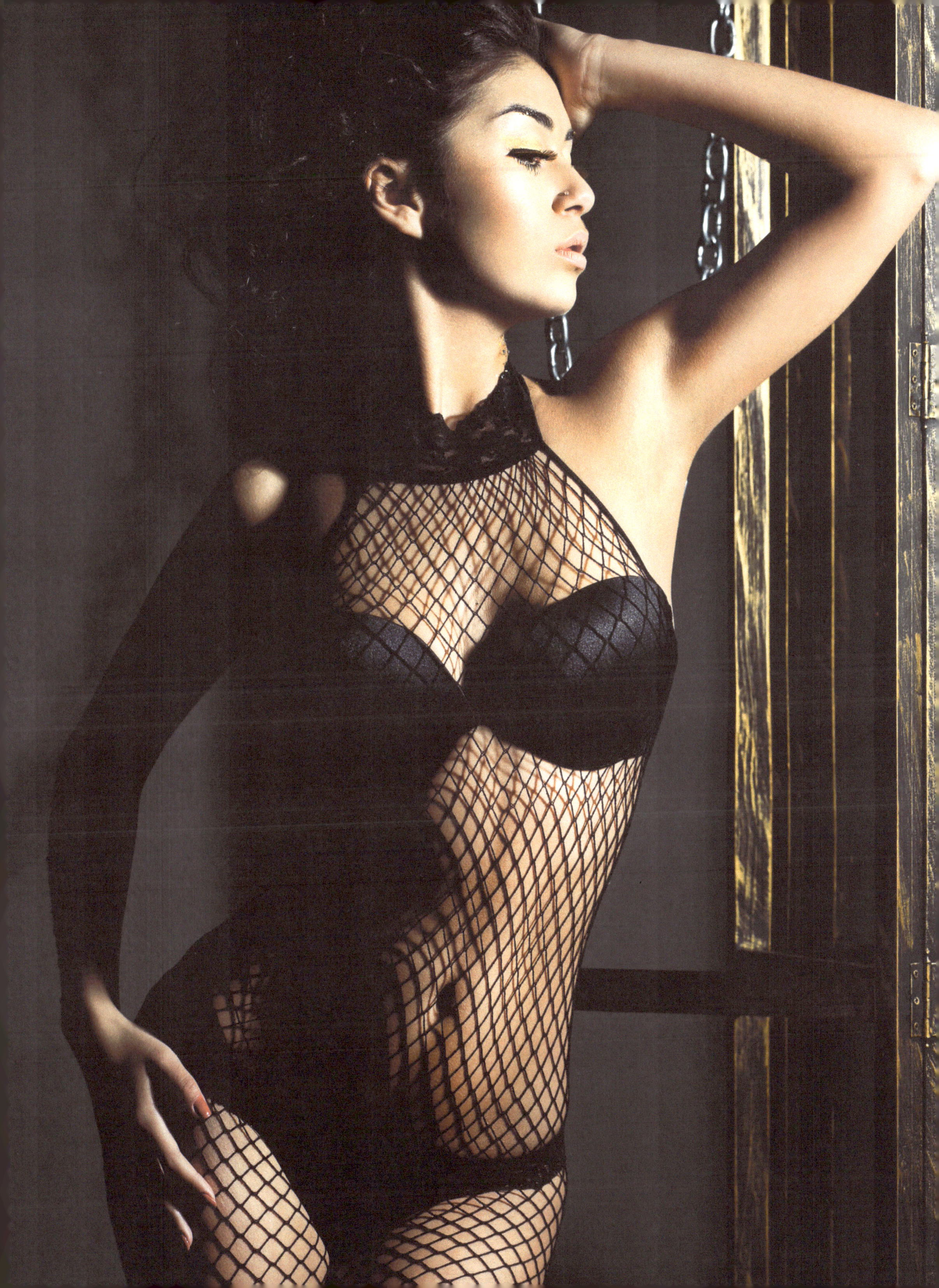

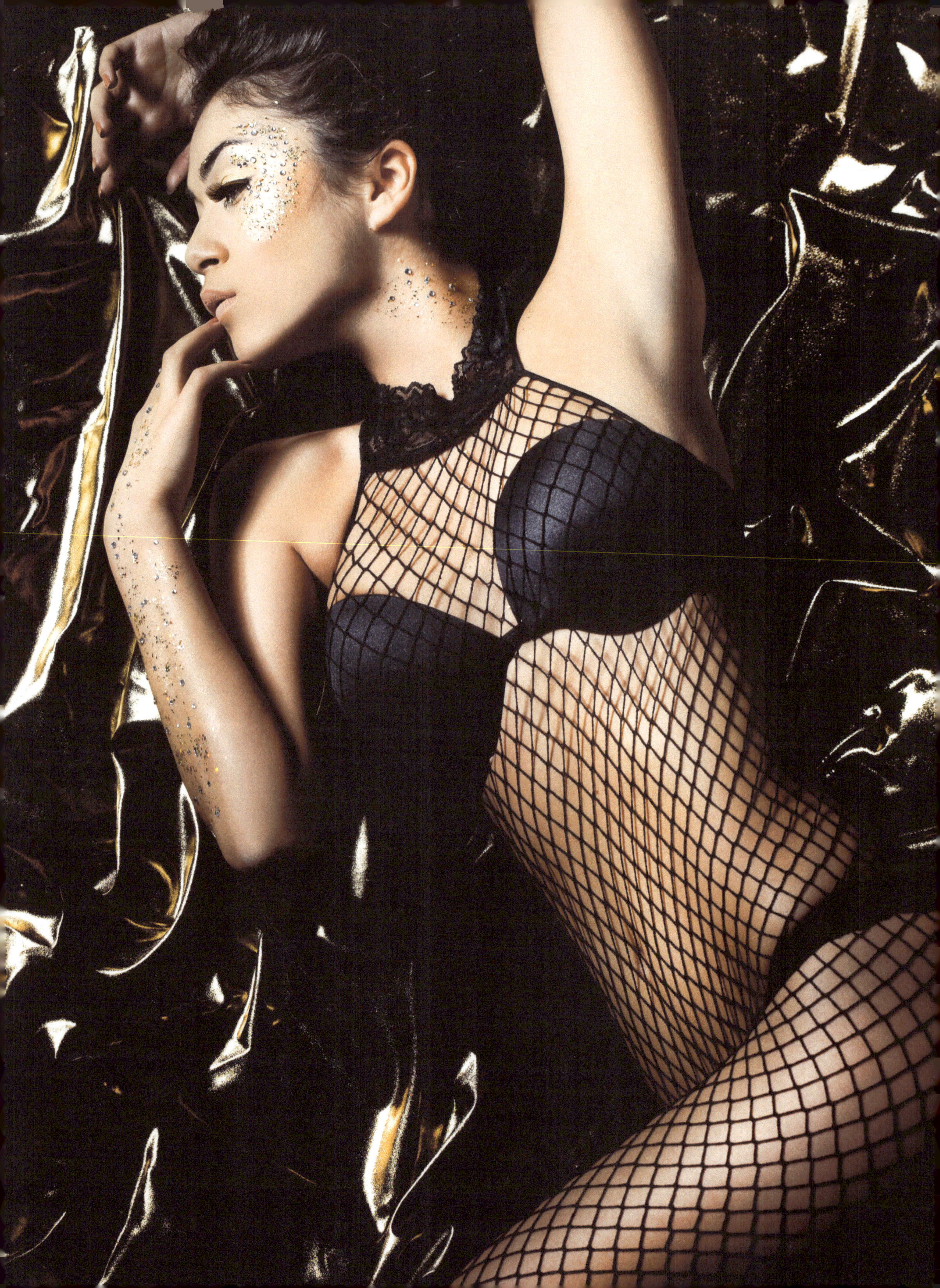

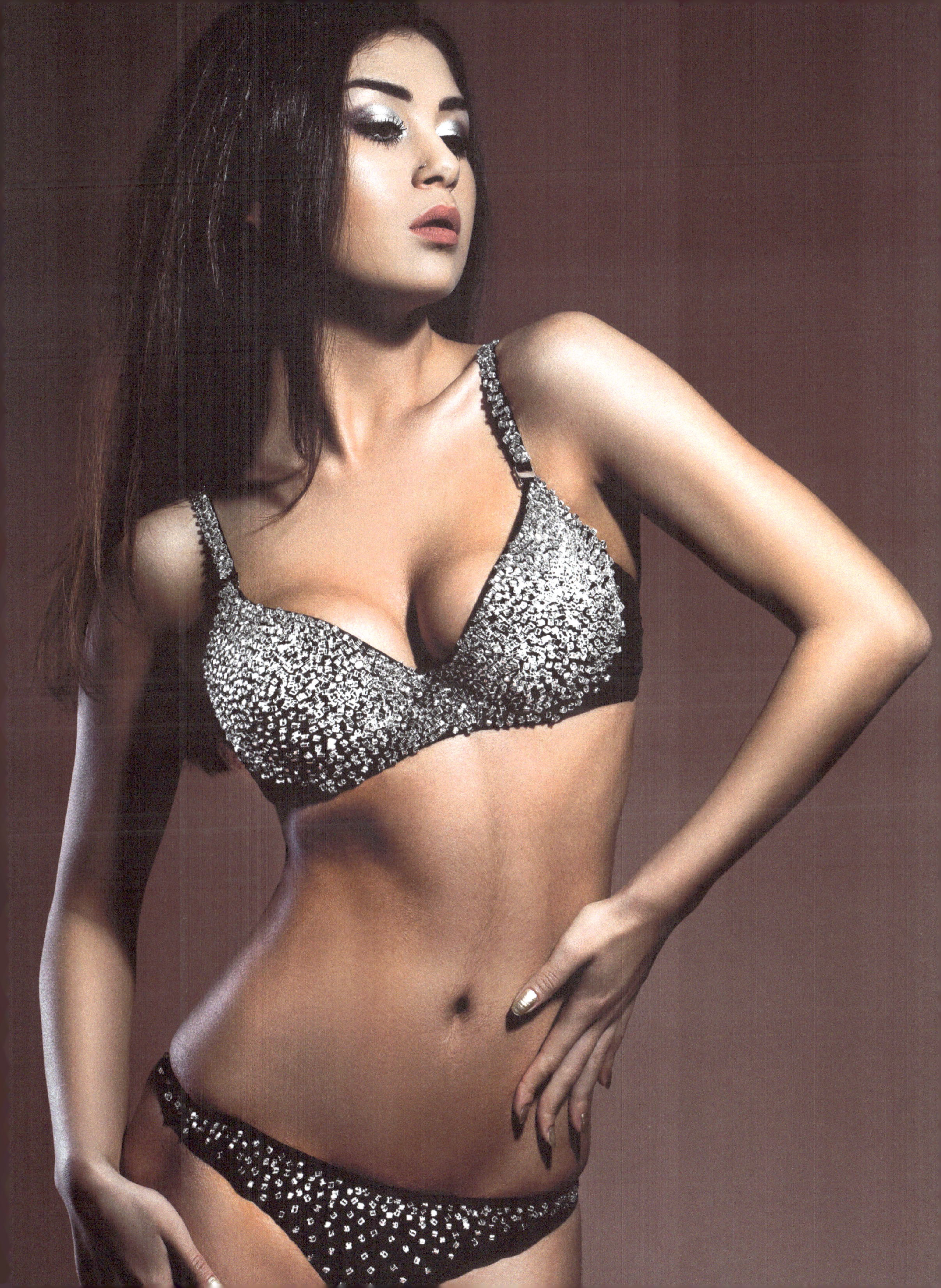

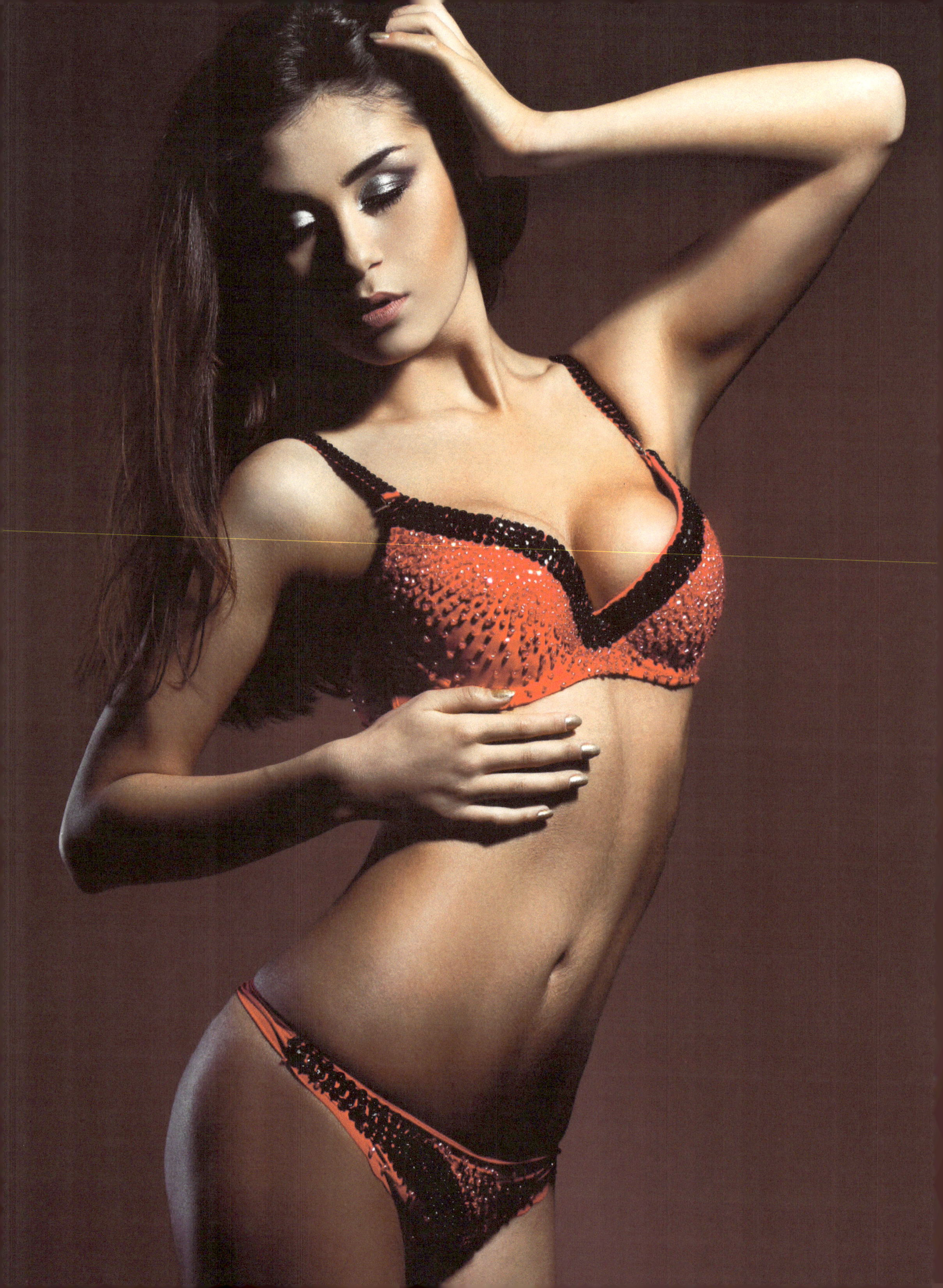

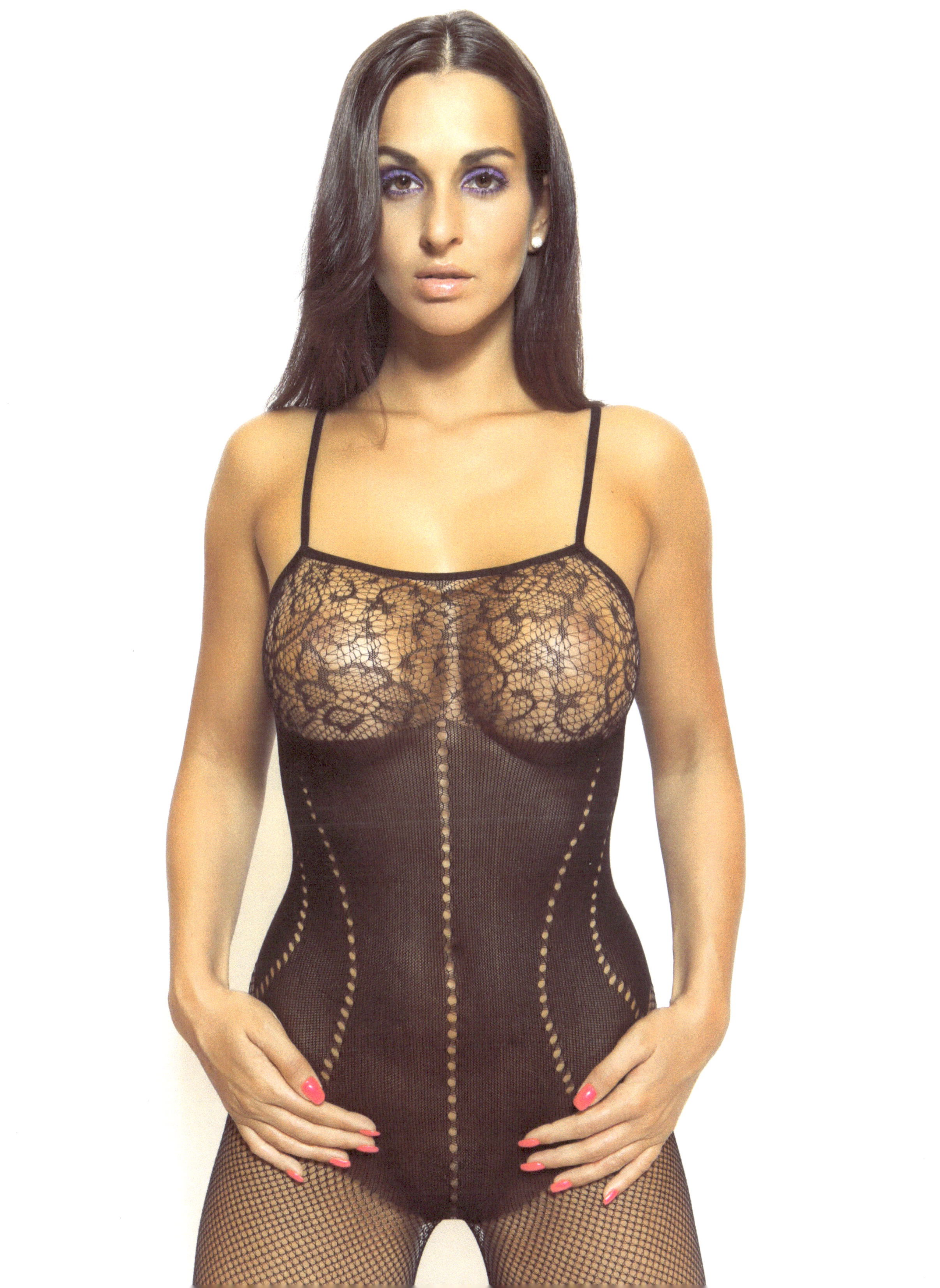

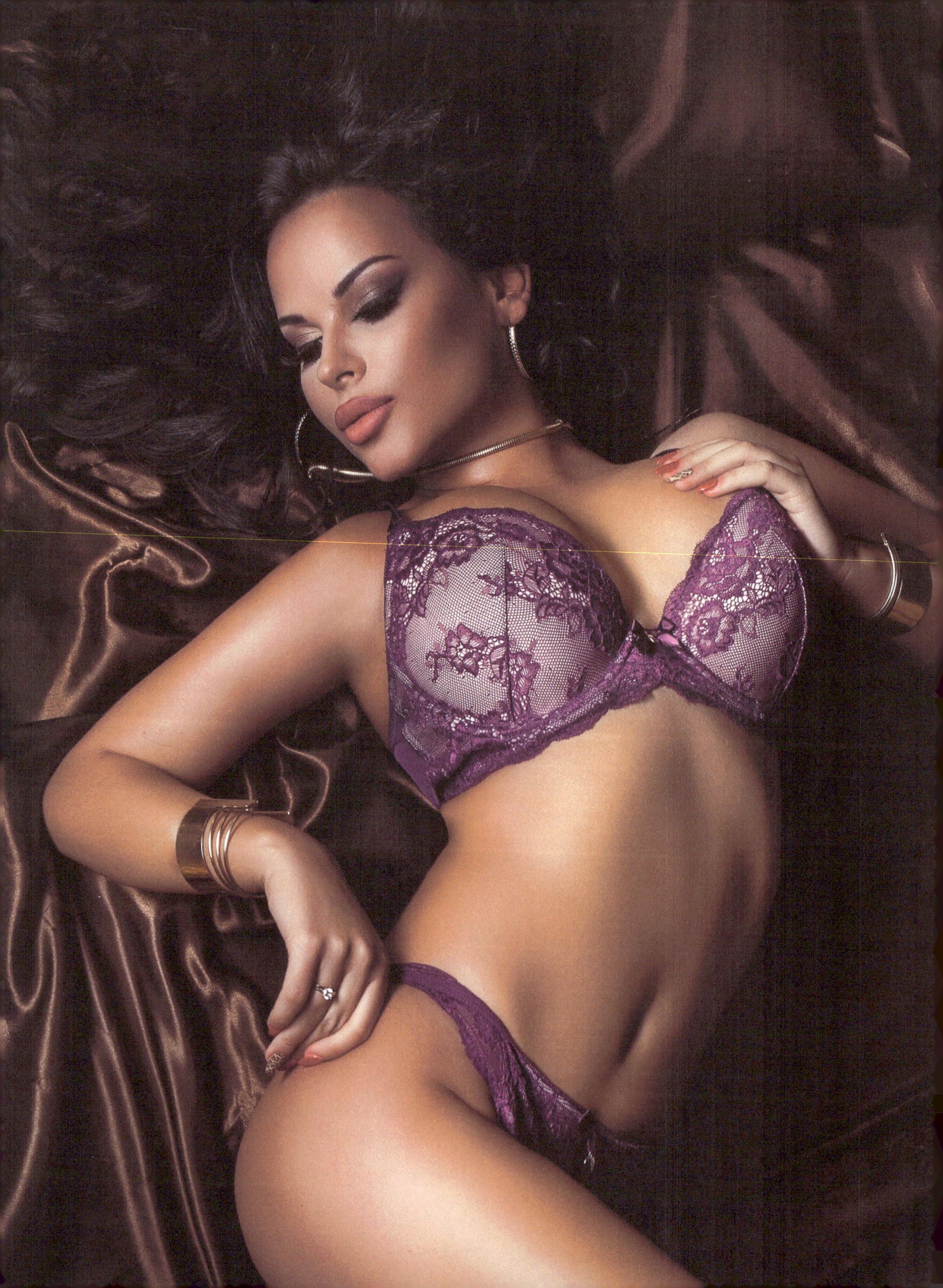

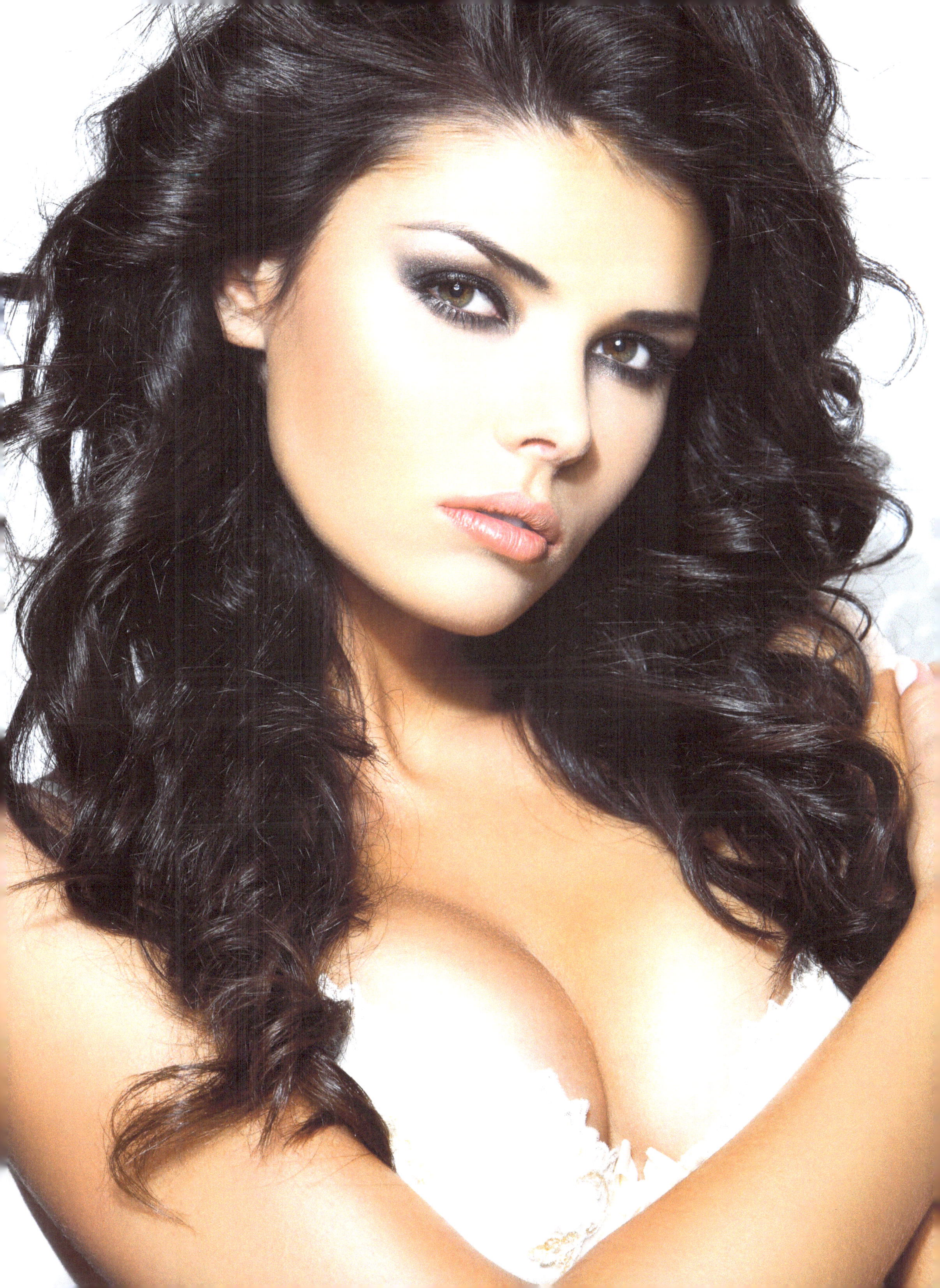

www.ingramcontent.com/pod-product-compliance
Lightning Source LLC
Chambersburg PA
CBHW050420180526
45159CB00005B/2340
* 9 7 8 1 5 3 9 9 1 4 0 7 5 *